Managing
Diversity

Pocket Mentor Series

The *Pocket Mentor* Series offers immediate solutions to common challenges managers face on the job every day. Each book in the series is packed with handy tools, self-tests, and real-life examples to help you identify your strengths and weaknesses and hone critical skills. Whether you're at your desk, in a meeting, or on the road, these portable guides enable you to tackle the daily demands of your work with greater speed, savvy, and effectiveness.

Books in the series:

Managing Diversity

Expert Solutions to Everyday Challenges

Harvard Business Press

Boston, Massachusetts

Library of Congress Cataloging-in-Publication Data

Managing diversity : expert solutions to everyday challenges.
    p. cm. — (Pocket mentor series)
  Includes bibliographical references.
  ISBN 978-1-4221-2880-0 (pbk. : alk. paper)
  1. Diversity in the workplace. I. Harvard Business Press.

  HF5549.5.M5M335 2009
  658.3008—dc22

                              2008039445

Contents

Tips and Tools   71

Tools for Managing Diversity   73

Worksheets to help you understand interpersonal bias, create an inclusive environment, develop a diversity profile of your team, conduct a recruitment interview, assess your cultural intelligence, and prepare for a cross-cultural business trip.

Test Yourself   87

A helpful review of concepts presented in this guide. Take it before and after you've read the guide, to see how much you've learned.

Answers to test questions   91

To Learn More   95

Further titles of articles and books if you want to go more deeply into the topic.

Sources for Managing Diversity   103

Notes   107

For you to use as ideas come to mind.

Mentor's Message: Why Learn to Manage Diversity?

Look around at your coworkers. How would you describe them? Do you observe much variety? Consider not only their physical traits but also their interests, skills, family backgrounds, physical abilities, religion, and other characteristics. Is your organization diverse? If not, it may be missing business opportunities at every turn.

Why? When a company builds a reputation for valuing differences, it attracts—and keeps—more talented employees. Diversity also helps companies do more than just generate new ideas in local markets. Employees with varied backgrounds can enable organizations to tap into global markets as well. With today's emphasis on globalization, that makes good business sense.

If you look around at your organization and see little variety, you'd probably benefit from adding diversity. This book shows you how. You'll start by learning how to dispel common misperceptions about diversity. Then you'll discover how to handle diversity-related conflict, foster an inclusive environment, and leverage the differences within your team. Additional sections show you how to recruit and retain diverse employees as well as strengthen your "cultural intelligence" for doing business across borders. The book concludes with a wealth of hands-on tools and practice opportunities for enhancing your diversity management skills.

Note, however, that this book is not intended as legal advice. If you encounter a diversity-related conflict that escalates in your team or department, *consult your human resources group and/or legal counsel.* They will be able to advise you on the specifics of your situation.

Martha R. A. Fields, Mentor

Martha R. A. Fields has close to thirty years of experience in management, human resources, and diversity/globalization. She is President, Founder, and CEO of Fields Associates, Inc., a firm that provides consulting, coaching, and educational programs in the areas of human resources management, executive development, diversity and globalization, and work/life integration. For six years, she chaired the Linkage Summit on Leading Diversity, the nation's premier diversity conference. Prior to starting her firm in 1994, she served as a vice president at a teaching hospital affiliated with Harvard Medical School. Martha is the former president of the Boston Human Resources Association and has received numerous awards, including the NorthEast Human Resources/Society for Human Resource Management's (SHRM) John D. Erdlen Five Star Award. She is a frequent keynote speaker and the author of the popular books *Indispensable Employees: How to Hire Them, How to Keep Them* and *Love Your Work by Loving Your Life (LwL²)*. Her latest book is *Roadmap to Success*, which she coauthored with Stephen Covey and Ken Blanchard.

Managing Diversity: The Basics

What Is Diversity?

As a manager, you've undoubtedly heard the term *diversity*. But what *is* diversity? *Diversity* is another word for differences between people. In an organizational setting, a diverse team or workforce comprises employees of various:

- Races

- Genders

- Ethnic backgrounds

- Ages

- Physical and cognitive abilities

- Sexual orientations and identities

- Religious beliefs

- Learning and work styles

- Body types

- Work/life commitments

When you build a diverse team in your department or unit, you provide your company with important advantages.

DIVERSITY *n* 1: The differences between people.

Why build a diverse workforce?

Many organizations encourage diversity because providing equal opportunity to everyone is the right thing to do. And in some countries, hiring and retaining a diverse workforce is also a matter of obeying antidiscrimination laws.

In addition, companies have discovered that a diverse workforce gives them important competitive advantages in the areas of talent recruitment and retention, employee commitment and productivity, and profitable innovation. When an organization builds a reputation for valuing differences, it often does better than its rivals at attracting and keeping talented employees. These individuals know that the company will appreciate and utilize the skills, backgrounds, and knowledge they bring to the table. And when employees use their differences to identify business opportunities and generate new ideas, they more fully express themselves at work. This leads to greater commitment and higher productivity.

Diverse workforces are thus rich seedbeds for new business ideas. For example, at one company, a disabilities task force thought of ways to make the firm's products accessible to people with physical limitations. As a result, the company won numerous contracts from government agencies that had a mandate to make accessibility of products a criterion in vendor selection.

The forces behind diversity

The competitive edge that a diverse workforce provides has become more essential than ever—owing to several key shifts in the business landscape. Take globalization. Many companies now operate in numerous regions and countries. To attract and motivate different employees from around the globe, as well as win and keep customers in a multitude of environments, managers must understand and demonstrate respect for cultural differences.

For instance, when a major American company set up a division in Spain, it initially provoked conflict with Spanish labor unions by expecting its Spanish employees to conform to American work schedules. Only after hiring Spanish managers for its new operation did the company regain workers' trust. With their greater understanding of Spanish culture, the new managers were more successful in negotiating mutually agreeable schedules with the employees.

"Diversity: the art of thinking independently together."
—Malcolm Forbes

Changes in the labor pool have also made workforce diversity more crucial than ever. Populations in many countries have grown more diverse, and labor pools reflect that diversity. For example, in the United States, Hispanics and Asians are the fastest-growing populations. And in France and Great Britain, Arab populations are rising. Organizations hoping to acquire the human resources they need to function must hire and motivate a wider variety of employees than before.

Finally, with change accelerating throughout the business world, companies are finding it increasingly difficult to stay ahead of the pack. By enabling employees to bring all of their unique qualities to work—including their differences—organizations stand a greater chance of maintaining an edge over rivals. To illustrate, in one consumer-products firm, a group of Mexican employees used their understanding of Hispanic culture and tastes to propose a new snack food that appealed to a previously untapped Hispanic market—and became a $100 million product.

The challenges of diversity

Though diversity offers major advantages, it can also present challenges. In particular, as people with very different beliefs, values, and priorities interact in the workplace, conflicts can arise.

Consider this example of how differences in work and non-work commitments can create tension: Paolo and Tamara are senior accountants who report to Stavros. Paolo recently negotiated an arrangement with Stavros to leave the office early on Fridays so he could spend more time with his children. Tamara, a dedicated churchgoer, asks Stavros whether she, too, can leave early once a week to attend a bible study class that's offered only on Friday afternoons. When Stavros says, "Sorry, no," Tamara concludes that he views her nonwork priorities as less important than Paolo's. Her resentment grows, and she begins to see company policies as unfair. Losing trust in Stavros and the company, she becomes reluctant to give her best on the job.

Some diversity-related conflicts arise from people's fear of being seen as prejudiced. For instance, Grace, a twenty-five-year-old manager, avoids giving needed constructive feedback to Bart, her fifty-year-old subordinate, fearing he'll accuse her of age discrimination. Bart thus never receives the information he needs to improve his performance on the job. In these kinds of situations, it's important for managers to determine whether they're dealing with a performance problem—or a diversity-related problem.

Steps for Distinguishing Between Performance- and Diversity-Related Problems

1. **Identify tension you're experiencing.** For example, Marc is concerned because James, an African American direct report, has recently delivered lower-than-usual performance levels on the job. Yet Marc is reluctant to give James critical feedback, for fear James will view him as racist.

2. **Define the job requirements of the person(s) in question.** For instance, the requirements of James's sales job include acquiring a specific number of new accounts per quarter.

3. **Ask whether the person(s) can fulfill the job requirements you've identified.** In James's previous job, with a different employer, he had similar job requirements, which he met or exceeded on a regular basis. His performance in this previous role was a major reason that Marc decided to hire James. Clearly, James is capable of fulfilling the job requirements.

4. **Separate facts from opinions about the problem at hand.** Marc identifies the following facts: James has met his job requirement during three of the past four quarters and exceeded those requirements during the first quarter. Marc also identifies an opinion: he has assumed that James's recent downturn in performance will continue or worsen.

5. **Consider whether there are any biases affecting views of the problem.** Marc finds himself recalling a time several years ago,

when he had hired an African American account manager who ultimately could not fulfill the requirements of the job in a consistent way. He realizes that that earlier experience is causing him to make assumptions about James's capabilities on the job—that he is overgeneralizing about James based on another experience.

6. **Identify actions needed to correct the situation.** Marc decides to talk with James about what has caused the recent downturn in his performance. Marc thinks it makes sense to offer James coaching to address the problem.

7. **Implement the actions you've identified.** By talking with James, Marc learns that a recent illness in the family has made it more difficult for James to devote as much energy to his job as he usually does. Marc discovers that James's elderly mother, who lives with him, has been diagnosed with an aggressive terminal illness. James now shares responsibility for her hospice care.

   While James used to handle e-mail and phone communications with customers during off-hours at his home office, he has been unable to do so for the last few months.

   Marc realizes that James's situation has nothing to do with his on-the-job abilities, and that the current dip in James's performance will likely prove temporary. He offers James his compassion and support and decides that no corrective action is necessary.

Adapted from Fields Associates, Inc., "Handling Differences Using the Fields Associates JOB-IT Model," 2006.

When these sorts of diversity-related tensions and fears escalate, productivity and morale can suffer. And organizations miss out on the advantages that diversity provides. You can surmount such challenges if you:

- Correct any misperceptions you might hold about difference.

- Deal effectively with diversity-related conflicts.

- Foster a workplace that embraces differences as much as similarities.

- Tap diversity's value.

- Recruit and retain a diverse workforce.

- Improve your ability to communicate with peers, employees, customers, and vendors from different cultures.

This book helps you achieve all of these goals.

Dispelling Misperceptions About Diversity

A S WE'VE SEEN, a diverse workforce gives any company important competitive advantages. For example, it enables the organization to attract and retain a variety of talented employees who generate creative ideas for new products and services. However, misperceptions about diversity can prevent companies from gaining these advantages by planting the seeds for conflict in the workplace. Let's examine these misperceptions and explore ideas for thinking differently about differences.

Members of a particular group aren't all alike

Some people tend to lump others under a label and assume that all members of a particular group or culture share the same characteristics. Such beliefs are *stereotypes*—conventional, formulaic, and oversimplified conceptions, opinions, or images of particular groups. Examples may include:

- "Asians are smart and hardworking."

- "Californians are laid-back when it comes to business."

- "Women have trouble with math."

- "Irish people love their drink."

- "Americans are pushy negotiators."

When stereotypes are negative, they constitute *prejudice*—defined as an adverse judgment or opinion formed beforehand or without knowledge or examination of the facts. Assuming that all members of a particular group are the same can have damaging consequences in the workplace. For instance, Sal, a manager at Marlon Pharmaceuticals, believes that women are less skilled at math than men. He decides not to promote Jessica, a talented employee, to a position requiring high-level math skills, because he assumes she'll have trouble in the new role. Jessica minored in math at college and has expressed interest in "working with numbers." After not getting the promotion, Jessica concludes that she has little opportunity for advancement at Marlon, and accepts a job offer from a competing organization.

The fact is, members of a particular group do *not* all necessarily share the same characteristics. To get the most from subordinates, managers must assess each employee's unique characteristics and strengths.

To dispel this misperception, identify the prejudices you hold about people different from you. Be honest with yourself, and challenge your beliefs. For example, recall individuals you know who do not fit stereotypes about their ethnic group, age, gender, or some other defining characteristic. Consider ways in which *you* don't fit stereotypes about a group of which *you're* a member.

What Would YOU Do?

Tapping a Top Team at TopCo

J ANICE HAS RECENTLY been hired as manager of an engineering department at TopCo. The company has long been committed to cultivating a diverse workforce, and Janice's new team reflects that diversity. Her on-site staff comprises men and women of various races and ethnicities. Janice's team also consists of a few engineers who work at satellite offices in other countries where TopCo is seeking to expand its markets.

Janice knows that part of her job is to ensure that TopCo benefits as much as possible from her team's diversity. And that means managing her employees' differences skillfully. She wonders how she might best approach the task as she eases into her new role.

What would YOU do? The mentors will suggest a solution in *What You COULD Do.*

"Difference is the essence of humanity."
—John Hume

Each person has *more* than one identity

Many people engage in either/or thinking about diversity. For example, perhaps you believe that in terms of their identity, people are *either* black *or* white, female *or* male, young *or* old, rich *or* poor, conservative *or* liberal, and so forth.

Either-or thinking causes people to define themselves *in opposition to* others—which can spawn conflict in the workplace. For instance, when Mahmoud, a high-achieving Muslim salesperson, is passed over for a promotion by David, his Jewish boss, he wonders whether discrimination was involved. He becomes critical around David, and their working relationship sours.

The fact is, every person has *multiple* identities. For instance, David is not just a Jew. He may also identify himself as a middle-aged man, a father, and an activist for liberal causes. He and Mahmoud may hold some of these identities in common. Perhaps, for instance, Mahmoud is also in his middle years, has children, and holds liberal views. By becoming aware of their shared identities, Mahmoud and David may feel less in opposition to each other. And they may forge a more positive, productive working relationship.

To practice imagining that people can have multiple identities, try this exercise: List *your* multiple identities, considering your home and personal life, as well as civic, professional, and other priorities. For example, "I'm a leader at my church, a marketing expert, and an animal rights activist." Now look for identities you share with other individuals at work. Likewise, encourage your subordinates to discover their similar identities and to learn about one another's differences and similarities.

A person's identity *can* change

Many managers assume that people's identities don't change, so they may neglect to offer their subordinates valuable developmental opportunities. To illustrate, Tanya has long managed the benefits group in the human resource department of Harrington Associates, a firm based in London. Her subordinates include Barry, an Indian-born benefits specialist who has reported to Tanya for many years. A year ago, while they were lunching together in the cafeteria and conversing about identities, Barry said to Tanya, "I see myself as a Hindu first, an HR professional second, and an Indian third."

When the company decides to establish a satellite office in India, Tanya never considers whether Barry might be interested in taking an overseas assignment at the new office. After all, he himself had placed his Indian background in last place in his list of identities during that earlier lunchtime conversation. Tanya doesn't realize that, in the past year, Barry's interest in his Indian heritage and culture has intensified and that he would welcome an opportunity to take on an assignment in India. Moreover, his interest in and familiarity with Indian culture would enable him to make a valuable contribution at the new office. Barry *and* the company lose out if Tanya isn't aware of changes in the way Barry identifies himself.

People's identities evolve as they acquire new experiences. To deepen your understanding of this, ask yourself how your own identities might be changing as you acquire new personal and professional experiences. Similarly, be open to the possibility that individual employees may see themselves in a different light as their life and work circumstances evolve. Avoid making assumptions about what each employee's priorities, interests, and goals might be, based on what you currently know about their identities. Take time during informal one-on-one conversations and performance reviews to find out how each employee's view of him- or herself may be changing. Consider what these changes imply for your direct reports' career aspirations.

Prejudice doesn't *always* come from majority members

Watch for any tendencies within yourself to judge or look down on someone else based on their age, gender, race, or some other defining characteristic. Many people assume that prejudice flows in one direction: from members of the numerical majority toward those in the minority or in positions of less power. However, prejudice can come from anyone and be directed toward anyone.

Consider the case of Herman, a sixty-year-old manager at Poulin Enterprises. He sometimes makes jokes about women during casual chats with colleagues at lunch. Martha, a thirty-one-year-old employee in the same department, has overheard a few of these jokes and finds them highly offensive. One day, Martha and Bette, a colleague, hear Herman telling another male manager that he's getting divorced. "Boy," Herman says, "all women are the same. They take everything we've got when they leave us, don't they?" Martha and Bette look at each other and roll their eyes. "The stupid old fool," Martha snaps, "it's about time his wife left him!" "I can't believe you have to work with him on that task force," Bette says. "Well, he's ancient and a typical male," Martha replies. "I don't take anything he says seriously."

Being aware of and correcting your misperceptions about differences are important first steps to building a workplace that values diversity. But it's not enough. In addition, you need to handle diversity-related conflicts effectively. The next section explores this topic.

What You COULD Do.

Remember Janice's concern about how to best leverage her team's diversity?

Here's what the mentor suggests:

To leverage her team's diversity, Janice must cultivate an inclusive environment—one that makes all employees feel welcome and encourages them to achieve maximum performance and productivity. Tools such as mentoring and incentives will help her foster this environment and retain her team's talent. She should also know how to resolve any diversity-related conflicts that may arise in her group, and be willing to identify and challenge any inaccurate assumptions she may hold about ethnic and other differences. She and her team will need to explore ways to avoid common cross-cultural communication gaffes. Moreover, given TopCo's multinational goals, Janice must consider how her employees can use their familiarity with different cultures to serve new customers.

Handling Diversity-Related Conflict

D IVERSE TEAMS MAKE better decisions than homogeneous ones, are more creative, and handle complex challenges more effectively. Yet diversity can also spark conflict. And when managers handle diversity-related conflicts poorly, talented performers flee in search of more welcoming environments. The result? The companies they've left fail to reap the benefits promised by diversity.

Understanding what it's like to feel "different"

One way to deal more productively with diversity-related tensions is to understand what it feels like to be "different"—to be a member of the numerical minority or in a position of relatively little power.

In some companies, members of the numerical majority (for example, white managers in an organization that employs few blacks) may hold prejudicial, deep-seated assumptions about members of the minority group. These assumptions can create a demoralizing climate of tension and distrust for minority members. Yet the majority members are unaware of this climate. Understanding what it's like to feel "different" in an organization can help managers handle diversity-related conflicts more effectively. Here are some examples of how minority members or people with relatively little power can be made to feel different by members of the minority:

- **"I feel like a token."** Some black managers suspect that whites can't see past blacks' skin color. For instance, at a management retreat, a newly hired African American vice president of strategic planning meets key decision makers. They express no interest in her business expertise. Instead, they ask her to head up the company's new diversity committee.

- **"I feel marginalized."** Racial minorities and women often feel relegated to the sidelines during important business discussions. For example, during a strategy meeting, Manuela, a department head, offers a suggestion for implementing a new competitive strategy. The room is quiet until a white male manager echoes Manuela's idea. The CEO then expresses interest in the idea. Concluding that others aren't willing to hear her thoughts, Manuela declines to contribute during future meetings.

- **"I feel I have to work harder to demonstrate my worth."** Managers who are members of the numerical majority can define expectations for others that feel demeaning or unreasonably stringent. To illustrate, when the leader of a small team comprising employees with college degrees hires several qualified people who have only a high school education, her boss begins requesting progress reports from these new hires that he'd never required before. The message? "I expect your team's performance to drop because of the new staff with less education." Though the newly configured team performs well, the director feels worn out by the pressure to constantly defend her employees' worth through meaningless reports. The following year, she accepts a position at a competing firm.

- **"I don't fully trust you."** Sometimes members of the numerical minority doubt that their majority-member colleagues will support them if they make a mistake. So they avoid taking risks. A case in point: After several drinks at a business dinner, Carla complains to Anton, her new colleague, that "homosexuals are always advocating their agenda." Anton is gay but has not told Carla about his sexual orientation. He decides to keep his distance from Carla—which hampers collaboration between their two departments.

Resolving the problem

When a diversity-related conflict arises, the person in the numerical minority may feel an intense need to be proved "right" about having experienced prejudicial treatment based on his or her minority status. Meanwhile, the individual in the numerical majority can experience an equally intense need to be "innocent" of committing an offense.

With such polarized needs, the two stand little chance of moving beyond the conflict. The following four steps can help you uncover what's fueling diversity-related tension between you and another person and how you might interact more productively.

- **Step 1: reflect.** If someone accuses you of prejudice, or you feel certain someone has shown prejudice toward you, pause to consider the facts of the situation and your goals before responding. For example, when Sondra's male law-firm colleagues joked that "things were much more fun here before so many women joined the firm," she checked her anger. Then she thought about how the incident could help her achieve a goal that mattered more to her than being "right." Sondra's goal? Enabling women to advance more easily to partner at the firm.

- **Step 2: connect.** Ask questions to better understand the other person's behavior and attitudes. Then share your own perspective. Sondra set out to understand what experiences lay under her male colleagues' disparaging humor about women. She asked them, "What was it like for you when women joined the firm? What did you feel you lost? Gained?" The men opened up, and Sondra explained the feelings that arose in her when well-meaning colleagues told unflattering jokes about women. The mutual openness diffused tensions and enabled everyone to focus once more on meeting important strategic goals. And in future meetings, Sondra was able to convince her colleagues that allowing women to advance more easily within the firm would benefit the entire organization.

- **Step 3: question yourself.** Ask yourself how your desire to be proved right about a perceived offense—or proved innocent of offending someone else—might have distorted your view of the situation. For instance, Edy, a thirty-nine-year-old manager, succeeded fifty-nine-year-old Brian as CEO at a consultancy. Brian, who remained as an adviser, told Edy that her push to market more vigorously to women in their thirties was "unwise." Though she initially took offense, Edy asked Brian to elaborate. He expressed concern that Edy's strategy would narrow the firm's market and alienate the current customer base of older men. Edy realized she needed to explain how her strategy would support the firm's mission. When she articulated her reasoning—and demonstrated her commitment to retaining current customers—Brian saw the value in her strategy. The tension between them eased, and Edy was able to move forward with implementing her new direction.

- **Step 4: shift your mind-set.** Ask yourself what changes you could make to improve your workplace relationships. For example, Richard, a French executive at a Paris-based consultancy, was frustrated with Suha, his Egyptian business partner. Richard saw Suha as controlling and critical when they took on major new consulting engagements. Rather than trying to persuade Suha to alter his behavior, Richard realized that the only thing he *could* change was himself. He initiated a conversation with Suha to learn more about his concerns. When Richard discovered that Suha's behavior stemmed from his worry about the firm's increasing workload, he agreed to shoulder more of the load. Their working relationship moved from prickly to positive.

Tip: Communicate high expectations of performance for all workers. Never hesitate to address an employee's lagging performance because you fear being seen as prejudiced.

Fostering an Inclusive Environment

HOW MIGHT YOUR organization reap the benefits of diverse workforces and teams—including increased access to new and existing markets, higher morale, and greater productivity? One powerful practice is to foster an inclusive environment.

In an *inclusive environment*, managers welcome the many differences that distinguish their employees, and they leverage them to define new goals, improve processes, and boost team productivity. Companies that cultivate an inclusive environment thus promote equal opportunity—while also valuing differences as much as they do similarities.

As employees in inclusive organizations see their unique characteristics generating positive business results, they feel valued precisely for what makes them special. As a result, their commitment to their jobs—and the company—grows.

Fostering an inclusive environment isn't easy, owing to two existing diversity approaches that get in the way. Think of these approaches as "assimilation" and "differentiation."

The disadvantages of assimilation and differentiation

In organizations that approach diversity through *assimilation*, people stress that "we're all the same." Assimilation promotes fair hiring, as managers strive to recruit diverse employees. This approach also has a major disadvantage: it encourages everyone to adhere to the corporate culture and codes of conduct defining how to look, act, and get ahead. This expectation of uniform behavior puts pressure on employees to downplay differences among themselves—which can carry a high price for their company.

Here's an example: Wu, a Chinese man who works in FreiCo's advertising department, believes that FreiCo's advertising strategy isn't appropriate for the Chinese marketplace. But he hesitates to cite his personal knowledge of Chinese culture in order to defend his opinion. Why? He fears that others will see him as importing inappropriate attitudes into an organization that prides itself on "sameness" and blindness to cultural differences. As a result, FreiCo never hears—or profits from—Wu's well-informed ideas.

In organizations that take a *differentiation* approach to diversity, people stress the fact that "we celebrate differences." Differentiation enables companies to expand into new and existing markets by matching diverse employees to niche customer segments distinguished by gender, race, age, ethnicity, socioeconomic status, and other defining characteristics.

However, differentiation also has an important downside: employees can feel they're being pigeonholed or exploited as tokens. They may also feel excluded from opportunities lying beyond the niche into which they've been slotted. Equally problematic, their ideas don't always get integrated into their company's mainstream work.

Consider this illustration: BestBank, a U.S. investment services company, has decided to aggressively expand into several Asian countries. To ensure that managers in the new offices have credibility with local customers and knowledge of local markets, BestBank hires Asians who live locally to manage its foreign offices. The new businesses prosper.

Yet BestBank as a whole never profits as much as it should have from this approach. Why? The bank's country teams all operate as spin-off companies, so no one in the home office can discern what makes the teams so successful. For instance, which investment banking practices would prove profitable only in particular cultures?

Because it followed a differentiated diversity strategy, BestBank won't learn from its country teams' best practices—and won't be able to put these practices to use in the larger organization. Moreover, BestBank has made itself vulnerable: if numerous managers from the Chinese team, for example, were to leave the company, BestBank would not know which skills to seek in successor managers. Thus the company might have difficulty re-creating its previous performance in that office.

Why inclusion is the best path

Because both assimilation and differentiation contain serious drawbacks, companies would do better to adopt a third approach that *transcends* the two existing ways. Many diversity experts think of this approach as *inclusion*.

In a company that fosters inclusion, employees' diverse perspectives are incorporated into the way business is conducted—changing things for the better.

Here's one illustration: Harmon & Hays, a small public-interest law firm based in Los Angeles, had an all-white legal staff that served an exclusively white female clientele. In light of the firm's mandate to advocate on behalf of all women, the attorneys were troubled by this homogeneity. To correct the situation, the firm hired Soledad, a Hispanic attorney.

Soledad brought in clients from her own community, demonstrating Harmon & Hays's commitment to serving all women. Even more valuable, she offered new ideas about which kinds of cases the firm should take on. For example, she suggested pursuing precedent-setting litigation that challenges English-speaking-only policies.

The firm had previously ignored such policies because they didn't fall under the purview of their traditional affirmative-action work. Soledad helped her colleagues see the link between English-only policies and employment issues for large groups of women—such as recent immigrants. These were potential clients that the company had earlier ignored.

Soledad thus expanded notions of what constituted "relevant" issues for the firm, and it started to see more immigrant clients. She enhanced not only the quality of Harmon & Hays's work but its ability to achieve its mission and to produce additional revenue.

Crafting a workplace of inclusion

One way to create a culture of inclusion is to foster open discussion of cultural backgrounds. For instance, a food company's chemistry department has employees from numerous different cultures. The department manager routinely expresses interest in the background of individual employees and engages them in conversation about their experiences. Li-Shen Chang, a Chinese chemist, is inspired to draw on his familiarity with Chinese cooking—not his scientific expertise—to solve a soup-flavoring problem that has been frustrating the department.

In an inclusive environment, managers demonstrate their belief that good ideas can come from anyone. For example, at TopCo, Janice has decided to launch a series of weekly planning breakfasts open to people from all hierarchical levels in the engineering department. With this move, she sends the message to her subordinates that she values their ideas—regardless of their differences or position in the department.

In inclusive, diverse workplaces, people share a broader range of ideas and feelings more frequently than they do in homogeneous organizations. Not surprisingly, this variety can spark tensions, and people may put forth perspectives that clash. To ensure that employees continue to feel safe in expressing themselves, set a tone of honest discourse.

For example, during one of the breakfast meetings, Janice observes that LaNita and Hank have opposing views on the department's proposed project plan. Janice responds to this situation by saying, "LaNita and Hank, you really seem to disagree about the direction our next project should take. Can you each say more about what's causing the intensity of your disagreement? And would you each describe your line of thinking in more detail, so we can agree on how to move forward?" By taking this approach, Janice has diffused a potentially explosive disagreement between two employees by acknowledging the tensions and resolving them swiftly and sensitively.

Steps for Creating an Inclusive Workplace Environment

1. Identify and challenge any assumptions you have about people from certain groups and their work abilities or attitudes. Inaccurate assumptions—stereotypes and prejudice—will negatively affect the way you interact with these individuals.

2. Communicate high expectations of performance for all workers. Never hesitate to address an employee's lagging performance because you fear being seen as prejudiced.

3. Soon after hiring new employees, find out whether they will need some reasonable and fair accommodation. For example, do they have religious holidays and practices that require accommodations at certain times during the year?

4. In providing examples to explain work assignments and concepts, draw from a variety of cultural reference points, not just your own experiences.

5. Spend time getting to know everyone on your staff. Let them know that you care about them as human beings, not just as workers.

6. Avoid telling jokes or making comments that reinforce stereotypes, and discourage others on your team from telling such jokes.

Adapted from Dr. Richard Fields, "How Managers Can Enhance Their Effectiveness by Creating and Sustaining an Inclusive Workplace Environment."

Tapping
Diversity's Value

T O MAXIMIZE THE business value offered by your team's diversity, think about how you might link that diversity to important business goals, apply diversity initiatives to all your employees, and challenge exclusionary beliefs that crop up in your group.

Linking diversity to business goals

To extract the most value from your diverse team, you need to enable every employee to perform to his or her full potential. That may require you to clarify the link between diversity and business goals. For instance, do you envision improving sales among existing customers? Expanding into new markets?

Now determine how diversity can help your team achieve those goals. Articulate your thoughts to your group. At one company, a product development manager told his employees, "Our goals include serving soon-to-be-retired individuals and women-owned start-ups. I need you to draw on your personal experiences to generate ideas for services that may appeal to them."

Don't assume that each employee knows how his or her unique talents can help bring about success. Ensure that your staff understand the organization's goals, and then discuss how each person can contribute to the achievement of those objectives.

By calling attention to differences among your subordinates and showing how this diversity can help the company reach strategic goals, you send the message that you value each employee's contributions. Equally important, you give every subordinate an opportunity to generate valuable business results.

Applying diversity initiatives to all employees

Envision diversity initiatives as encompassing *all* employees—not just members of minority groups. For example, suppose you're a manager working in the Northeast region of the United States. If your goal is to assemble a team representing a wide range of ethnicities, genders, ages, and abilities, don't ignore forty-five-year-old white males. Omitting them from the team would be just as exclusionary as leaving out representatives from minority groups. Moreover, like any other demographic category, forty-five-year-old white males constitute a potentially profitable market.

Indeed, before implementing any diversity effort, ask yourself a key question: "Will this initiative contribute to *everyone's* success in my team? Or will it produce an advantage for only one or certain groups?" The most valuable diversity initiatives benefit everyone. For instance, assembling a task force to explore ways for a minority ethnic group to advance more easily in your unit ultimately helps everyone. Why? Generally, the more diverse the unit's leadership ranks become, the more creative ideas they will generate for improving processes or better serving customers. The more creatively your unit operates, the more successful it becomes—which can lead to rewards for everyone.

*"We need diversity of thought in the world
to face the new challenges."*

—Tim Berners-Lee

Exposing and challenging exclusionary beliefs

Beliefs about the personal qualities required to get ahead in your company can bar certain groups from opportunities to be hired *and* to give their best on the job. By exposing and challenging these beliefs, you remove those obstacles so that your company can extract more value from differences.

To illustrate, at InfoTech, which employs mostly men, one manager cited "ability to work with people" and "compassion" as prerequisites for promotion to leadership positions. But then he admitted, "That's the *official* story. In truth, it's aggressiveness that *really* gets people hired and promoted here. And most women just don't have that trait."

At InfoTech, the belief that women can't be "aggressive" blocks qualified female employees from being hired and advancing to leadership positions. To hire and promote more women—and thereby gain the benefits that diversity offers—managers at InfoTech would need to first reexamine their actual criteria for promotion, asking, "Do aggressive leaders truly get better results than compassionate ones?" They would also benefit from challenging their beliefs about women, asking, "Are most women really incapable of being aggressive when the need arises?"

In addition to the above suggestions, addressing the unique challenges of recruiting diverse employees can help you further tap diversity's power. The next section turns to this topic.

"If we cannot end now our differences, at least we can help make the world safe for diversity."
—John F. Kennedy

Recruiting a Diverse Team

MANY MANAGERS ENCOUNTER frustrating obstacles in trying to recruit a diverse team. For example:

- "I've looked for diverse job candidates, but I just can't find many in this area."

- "The HR department found diverse candidates for a position, but I wasn't confident that they were the best qualified for the job. I don't want to hire diverse team members just for the sake of diversity."

- "Though we have diversity in our hourly paid workforce, there's little of it in the middle and senior management ranks. Qualified diverse candidates are shying away from our company because they don't see anyone at the top who looks like them."

How to surmount these challenges? You may need to stretch beyond your usual recruiting tactics in order to find diverse, qualified candidates and persuade them to join your team. The following ideas can help.

Expanding your recruiting strategies

If you're having trouble recruiting additional diverse team members, consider using multicultural marketing approaches to identify the media through which people from different cultural groups get their information. Some examples of media outlets could be:

- Ethnic radio and TV stations
- Community newspapers
- Trade journals
- The Internet

Once you've identified each group's preferred media, advertise job openings in those media for each group you're targeting. Also, join forces with organizations or key community leaders that service the social, civic, religious, and educational needs of the groups whose representation you're seeking to improve in your team.

Tip: To recruit diverse new hires, visit multicultural-oriented Web sites and diversity focused e-zines used by groups you're interested in hiring. You'll learn more about their career interests, and you can post job advertisements in these venues.

For instance, suppose you want to recruit additional people of color in your department. You discover that a local community center runs a weekend program for young people of color on how to plan their careers. You invite one of your direct reports to give a

What Would YOU Do?

Allergic to Homogeneity

L UC HAS BEEN ASKED to lead a special team charged with selling his company's products to consumers with food allergies. He knows that such allergies are more prevalent in some groups than others. For example, lactose intolerance is high in African American and Latino populations in the United States. And peanut and other nut allergies are growing more common among children.

Luc knows that his team is fairly homogeneous. He's worried that without a more diverse group, he'll have difficulty fulfilling the team's mission. But in the past, Luc has had difficulty recruiting people of color and working mothers—two groups he thinks would help the team significantly on this project. How can he recruit these diverse candidates?

What would YOU do? The mentors will suggest a solution in *What You COULD Do.*

---

short presentation on career management to attendees at the program. The payoff? You get your company's name out to the local community, and you identify possible future hires for your department.

Seeking assistance from within your company

Your company's current employees can also help you recruit a diverse team. Individuals within your organization who represent groups you're interested in recruiting may know qualified individuals who fit your desired profile. Suggest that your organization create an employee referral bonus program, whereby employees would get rewarded for finding qualified diverse job candidates, if such a program does not already exist.

Your organization may also benefit from the power of employee affinity groups. Suggest to your HR department or senior leadership that members of diverse groups throughout your organization form groups to "sell" your company to potential job candidates. For example, an indigenous peoples' group could talk with candidates as well as community and educational groups about your organization, what it's like to work there, and how they've advanced in the company.

Tip: To get the most out of employee affinity groups, point out to HR the value of requiring that all affinity group activities have a business outcome. Such outcomes could include professional development of members, recruitment of diverse job candidates, or marketing of your company's image to targeted consumers.

"Selling" your company to potential new hires

It's not enough to locate potential diverse new hires; you also have to persuade qualified candidates to work for you. The following techniques can help:

- **Tout your company's progress in hiring for diversity.** Even if the organization overall still has a way to go in its diversity efforts, point out to qualified candidates what you've achieved so far. For example, "We've increased the percentage of women in middle and upper management from 35 percent to 45 percent over the past two years. We know we need to do more, but we've made a good start and are working to correct things." You might also let them know about future initiatives the organization plans to implement.

- **Emphasize the advantages of working for your organization.** If your department or company offers advantages over rival organizations, explain those advantages to diverse job candidates. For instance, perhaps you foster employees' career development by offering them special "stretch" assignments that enable them to strengthen their skills. Or maybe you've defined job roles and work schedules in such a way that everyone in your department is able to balance his or her work and personal or family commitments.

Once you've recruited diverse employees, your work doesn't stop there. You also need to retain them. Let's take a closer look at that task next.

What You COULD Do.

Remember Luc's question about how best to recruit diverse members for his team?

Here's what the mentor suggests:

For starters, Luc could think about how people in the groups he wants to target generally gather information and news. That way, he can put his job postings where people will see them. For example, there may be some ethnic radio stations, targeted news Web sites, local newspapers, and online job boards catering to specific populations that would make good candidates for his postings.

But purchasing targeted media spots may not be enough. Luc should also ask coworkers and friends whether they know qualified individuals who fit his desired profile. In addition, he might recruit from universities with a high ratio of women, people of color, and other diverse groups. To use this strategy, he could have representatives from his department participate in career-day activities and multicultural initiatives at these schools.

Once Luc identifies promising candidates, he may need to "sell" the company to them—that is, convince them that they're making the right choice in joining his organization. To do so, he could point out some of the advantages of working for the organization that may appeal to these candidates. These advantages might include special assignments that enable employees to strengthen and broaden their skills. They may also include company policies that help employees balance their work and personal lives—such as telecommuting, flexible health- and dependent-care spending accounts, elder- or child-care assistance, or domestic-partner benefits.

Retaining Diverse Employees

ECRUITING THE DIVERSE employees you need to help your company stay competitive isn't enough. You also have to *keep* them. Retention can be challenging. This is especially true if the employees you've recruited don't feel welcomed and appreciated or if they have not advanced in their careers. Recently recruited employees may also leave if they've come from other countries and have difficulty understanding your company's culture and/or work standards.

To retain members of your diverse team, you may need to reexamine your human capital systems to see whether they would benefit from revision. These systems include incentives, work/life programs, professional development initiatives, performance appraisals, and mentoring mechanisms.

Reexamining incentives

Start by taking a look at the incentives—financial and nonfinancial—you use to reward your team. Ask yourself, "Do these incentives send the message that we value diversity in this group? Do they encourage people to learn about one another's differences and use them to improve business processes and achieve important goals? Are they valued by all members of my staff?"

For example, a weekend getaway for two as a reward for good performance may be ideal for some members of your staff. But it wouldn't be as useful for employees with several children who may be reluctant to spend a weekend away from their kids—and who would have to take on the extra expense of hiring a babysitter.

On the basis of your answers to the above questions, consider how you might change your incentive systems to better retain your diverse team. If money is tight, think about nonfinancial or low-cost rewards—such as the opportunity to head up a major project, attend a conference, or participate in an in-house professional development seminar of interest.

Tailoring work/life programs

Offer a range of policies to suit the diversity of your employees' work/life needs. For instance, Lourdes, a manager at Prime Co., knew that a disproportionate number of her company's employees in their forties and fifties shouldered responsibility for their immediate families *and* their extended families. To save these employees from burnout, Lourdes began offering flextime and telecommuting for subordinates who had job responsibilities that could be carried out at any time and from any location.

In tailoring your work/life programs, make sure that one group's work/life needs don't overshadow another's. For example, don't always depend on young, single employees to shoulder workloads of individuals who regularly leave early for family commitments.

Also, make sure that your approach to work/life integration matches what you told candidates during job interviews. Too many managers tout their company's commitment to work/life balance in order to win talented new employees—without taking into account that this commitment varies across departments. A newly hired employee accepts the job offer and then learns that, owing to the nature of their assignments, people in his department work longer hours than employees in most other departments.

Developing employees' professional skills

Help diverse subordinates use their unique experiences to hone their on-the-job skills and advance in their careers. To illustrate, suppose you discover that Victor, a devout Catholic in your unit, volunteers for fund-raising at his neighborhood church and manages several youth groups in his off-hours. Through talking with him about these civic commitments, you realize that Victor has acquired some valuable skills—namely, strategic planning, change management, negotiation, and financial savvy. These abilities are essential for an upcoming special project in your department.

You encourage Victor to extract lessons from his community work and apply them in stretch assignments on the job. For example, you invite him to head up a task force charged with introducing a new customer service process to your team. This opportunity helps *Victor* further strengthen his change management skills. And it enables your *department* to improve its processes and enhance customer loyalty.

Customizing performance appraisals

Customize developmental goals introduced through performance appraisals to each employee's unique circumstances. For example, during Victor's next performance appraisal meeting, you invite him to sign up for an internal training course that helps new managers further strengthen their leadership skills.

Here's another illustration: Suppose that Dianna, a new mother who works in your unit, has negotiated a reduced workweek (with corresponding reduction in pay) so she can spend more time with her infant son. When conducting your annual performance appraisal for Dianna, allow for her part-time status while evaluating her on-the-job results. That is, don't expect her to produce the same volume of work in a thirty-two-hour week that a forty-hour-a-week employee in the same job would produce. Instead, focus the performance appraisal on how well she met the goals, deadlines, and quality requirements in her negotiated agreement.

Establishing mentors

Identify mentors who can provide diverse employees with instruction, coaching, and long-term, close developmental support as they progress through their careers. Mentors can come from within your department or from outside sources, such as other teams in the organization or external professional associations. Mentors from outside your functional area may be able to offer their protégés broader perspectives on the workings of the company.

Some employees may benefit from mentors who are similar in age or who come from the same ethnic group. Others may prefer mentors with a different perspective or background. Both have benefits. For example:

- **Mentors with different backgrounds.** A mentor who has a different background from his or her protégé can often help that person understand what it is like to be a member of the mentor's group. For instance, consider a white male who is a senior executive at a manufacturing plant. He is mentoring a female African American middle manager who is struggling in her management of an assembly line composed primarily of white males. As her mentor, he may be able to help her deal with employees' resistance to her ideas by sharing some of his own experiences with leading change.

- **Mentors with similar backgrounds.** Matching mentors with protégés from the same groups can offer unique benefits as well, such as enabling protégés to feel a greater sense of camaraderie and support. If it's impossible to find the ideal match for a particular employee, try to identify mentors who understand and appreciate the unique career challenges faced by the particular employee in question, as well as his or her special contributions.

To illustrate, perhaps Jon, a white employee in the marketing group, would make an excellent mentor for Taja, your Pakistani-born employee. That's because Jon's sister-in-law, Mikela, was born to Pakistani immigrants. Over the years, Jon has watched as Mikela has encountered challenges but nevertheless advanced through her career as a product developer. Because Jon is familiar with Mikela's experiences, he can support Taja as she progresses along her professional path.

Spotlight on Cultural Diversity

CHANGING HUMAN-CAPITAL systems to retain your diverse team can help you get the most value from the differences among your subordinates. Sharpening your understanding of the cultural diversity that characterizes today's globalized business world is also important. In this section, we take a closer look at this subject.

What is culture?

In today's age of global business, you probably hear the word *culture* used often. But what *is* culture, exactly? A person's culture determines his or her:

- Beliefs—about how the world works and how people should interact

- Behaviors—including gestures, use of eye contact, facial expressions, manner of dress, and rituals for greeting

- Values—what's considered important, such as family or personal life, career, religion, and social responsibility

Culture can be defined not only at a national level but also at the regional, organizational, or group level. For example, people living and working in the American Northeast and Southeast may have different beliefs, behaviors, and values (*regional* cultural differences). People in a large consumer-products corporation may have a very different culture from people who work for a small, not-for-profit entity (*organizational* cultural differences). And people who work in a marketing department may do business differently from those who work in the information technology function (*group* cultural differences).

Given the increase in international business that many organizations are experiencing, this topic focuses primarily on national and regional cultural differences.

CULTURE *n* **1:** The beliefs, behaviors, and values held collectively within a group, organization, region, or nation.

How is culture expressed?

Culture influences virtually all aspects of business. For example, people from different cultures may carry out the following activities in very different ways:

- Negotiating

- Communicating about business and nonbusiness topics

- Building working relationships

- Resolving conflicts

- Defining work procedures and ethical behavior

- Making decisions

- Greeting one another

- Establishing deadlines and meeting times

- Dressing

- Entertaining and dining

- Delivering presentations

- Evaluating business ideas and proposals

- Setting business priorities

- Relating to authority figures

- Selling and marketing to customers

When people from different cultures do business together, misunderstandings can result. For example, Malcolm, a manager at a New York firm, travels to Tokyo to negotiate a sales deal with a customer. That evening, he and several managers from the Tokyo firm meet for dinner. As cocktails are served, Malcolm begins discussing the deal's details. He doesn't realize that in many Asian cultures, people often prefer to establish relationships through nonbusiness conversation first. The Tokyo team members exchange uncomfortable glances and remain quiet during the rest of the evening. Malcolm returns to New York with no deal in hand.

"If we are to achieve a richer culture, rich in contrasting values, we must recognize the whole gamut of human potentialities."
    —Margaret Mead

Strengthening your "cultural intelligence"

Possibilities abound for misunderstandings based on cultural differences. How do you avoid business gaffes based on cultural misunderstandings? Strengthen your *cultural intelligence (CI)*—your ability to adapt to a new cultural setting, learn patterns of social interactions specific to that setting, and respond in ways considered appropriate by people from that culture.

By emulating others' cultural "rules" when interacting with them, you demonstrate your respect for them and for how they conduct business in their own culture. They respond by becoming more trusting and open—essential ingredients in any business interaction.

To build your CI, you can read books and articles or view videos and DVDs about cultural differences, as well as attend events and activities specific to particular groups. You can also get help from a coach specializing in cultural diversity, or simply begin to foster relationships with people from groups that are different from yours. They can help you better understand and navigate your way through their culture.

In addition to educating yourself on other people's cultures, you can also master these three components of CI:

- Use your *head* to observe and learn about others. Look for clues to a culture's shared understandings. For example, suppose you're about to take part in a series of meetings with a negotiating team from another country. During your early encounters with members of the team, observe their attitudes toward time. (Are they always punctual—or "fashionably" late?) Watch behavior regarding deadlines. (Do they stick to them rigidly—or treat them as "guidelines"?) Observe their use of language. (Do they bluntly say no to proposals they consider unacceptable—or merely smile and say they'll "get back to you" and then not respond?)

- Use your *body* to emulate others. Seventy percent of communication is through body language. Practice mirroring the customs and gestures of people from other cultures. For example, do they greet one another with a handshake or with a kiss to both cheeks? Do men never shake women's hands, and vice versa? While chatting, are they "up close and personal," or do they stand several feet apart? How much—if any—eye contact do they make? Under what circumstances do they smile or bow?

- Use your *heart* to believe you can learn about others. Embrace the notion that you are capable of understanding people from other cultures. In the face of obstacles, setbacks, or outright failure, strive with even greater rigor to familiarize yourself with others' cultures, and follow their norms when you're in their territory.

Understanding a culture does not mean you must embrace all its beliefs and behaviors. Neither does it imply that you must change your values or indulge in a cultural practice that you disagree with. What it *does* mean is that you use your knowledge of others' culture to understand why they do business the way they do. This understanding can lead to more positive, productive relationships in the workplace and with your customers.

Tip: When doing business with people from another culture, let the people you're meeting with set the pace for introducing, discussing, and negotiating business issues. Show individuals from the other culture your interest in learning about their lives. Ask appropriate questions, and listen to the answers.

With the increased globalization of business—including off-shoring, setting up operations in various countries, and establishing far-flung virtual teams—international cultural differences have presented managers with particularly daunting challenges. To successfully manage cultural diversity around the globe, managers must be especially savvy communicators. The next section examines cross-cultural communication more closely.

"In order to appreciate the cultures of another nation, one needs to go there, know the people, and mingle with the culture of that country."
—David Rockefeller

Communicating Across Cultures

N TODAY'S BUSINESS world, most large organizations operate globally. They sell their products and services to customers from various countries, employ individuals from different nationalities, and use suppliers from around the world. They compete against rivals coming from many points on the globe, forge joint-venture partnerships with companies in other countries, and assemble virtual teams comprising employees from far-flung locations.

If your company operates in any of these ways, you can expect to routinely encounter and communicate with people with national cultures different from your own. For example, you may be asked to:

- Form a virtual team made up of employees from different countries and time zones, and lead the team from your home office or an overseas location.

- Visit a customer in another country and negotiate an important deal.

- Meet with potential vendors from different countries to discuss their services and select the right supplier for your firm.

- Travel to another country and meet with representatives from a joint-venture partner to discuss progress on a major project.

In all of these scenarios, you can't assume that you'll interact and communicate with people from other cultures the same way you do at home. Indeed, if you expect individuals from other countries to negotiate, discuss business, and resolve problems exactly as you do, you risk committing communication gaffes that can sour your business relationships and hurt your company's—and your—performance.

Avoiding communication gaffes

Operating globally can benefit all the parties involved. But cross-border cultural differences can make communication difficult. How to avoid gaffes while communicating with people from other countries? The following ideas can help:

- **Sharpen your awareness.** Hone your awareness—and appreciation—of the vast differences in communication styles among national cultures by taking advantage of resources provided by your company or online, such as books and articles on the subject as well as experts.

- **Use your "people skills."** Draw on your people skills by observing others and adapting to their communication styles. Keep your awareness of national culture differences in mind while interacting with others. However, don't overgeneralize by assuming that two people from the same culture communicate in identical ways. Look for each person's individual style as well.

- **Get educated.** Take advantage of any cross-cultural training and coaching provided by your company. If your organization doesn't provide such resources, consider obtaining them yourself through online programs or courses offered by local colleges and continuing education programs.
- **Find "cultural mentors."** Identify peer managers in your firm who you see as particularly skilled at cross-border communication. Ask them what they do to enhance their ability to communicate with people from other nations. Then practice applying their methods to your own cross-border dealings.

Watching for language-based misunderstandings

Often, people from different countries use English to discuss business together. But because comprehension of English can vary greatly, misunderstandings may occur. For example, Larry leads a virtual team charged with designing brochures for new products. One morning, he e-mails Maya, a newly hired freelance graphic artist based overseas. In his e-mail, he asks her when she'll have the mock-up ready to circulate among the team members.

By *mock-up*, Larry is referring to a rough draft of the brochure, showing placement of text and photos. Maya understands *mock-up* to mean a more finished version of the brochure. So, she tells him she'll have it ready in two weeks. Larry thinks to himself, *What? Two weeks to do a mock-up?* Because Larry doesn't realize that he and Maya are defining *mock-up* differently, he becomes skeptical of Maya's abilities and starts micromanaging her. Eventually, their relationship sours, corroding the team's morale and productivity.

Language-based misunderstandings can arise from nonverbal differences as well. People from different countries use body language to mean different things. These nonverbal signals include gestures, silence, touch, eye contact, and facial expressions. If you don't understand the different meanings assigned to such signals, you may misread them in another person.

For instance, suppose you've been assigned to lead a project team for several months in another country where your company has set up a satellite office. Soon after you arrive at the new location, you meet with each team member individually to introduce yourself and discuss project plans. During these meetings, you notice that a number of the team members make very little eye contact with you. You don't realize that in their country, looking an authority figure in the eye signifies lack of respect. In your country, lack of eye contact suggests deception. So you interpret their behavior incorrectly—concluding that they're trying to conceal something from you. The project starts off unnecessarily on a note of mistrust.

Negotiating across cultures

Negotiation styles vary widely across cultures. In some countries, negotiators open talks by emphasizing the negative aspects of the bargaining so far; in others, the positive. Some believe that withholding information is power. Some consider it rude to say no outright. People may also have very different preferences for how to set the pace of discussions during a negotiation.

To illustrate, Reed, a manager for a company based in Los Angeles, meets with Khoa, a manager at a Hanoi-based supplier, to negotiate a potential contract. For Reed, negotiation is about pushing through a deal—period. When Reed decides that the discussion isn't moving forward as quickly as he thinks it should, he presents increasingly forceful arguments. Khoa, who typically first builds a relationship with his negotiation counterpart and then slowly enters into the bargaining, interprets Reed's behavior as disrespect. Their negotiation fizzles, and what could have been a mutually beneficial deal never comes to pass.

What constitutes an agreement also affects cross-cultural negotiation, because it hinges tightly on cultural norms. For some cultures, a verbal agreement is sufficient for both parties to move ahead with implementing a deal. In others, bargainers require formal legal documents to consider an agreement sealed. Lack of understanding of these different norms can lead to painful misunderstandings and lost business.

Consider this example: You work for a small start-up that's developing a new technology. You've met with several engineers and marketers from TechInc, a potential customer from another country, to gauge TechInc's interest in your product. At each meeting and during each phone call, you hear comments from the TechInc representatives such as, "We're definitely on board, and we'll want to get the work done as quickly as possible. We'll get the purchase order to you by the end of next week."

You assume that this verbal agreement means you'll actually receive the purchase order by the designated date. Mindful of TechInc's urgency about having the order filled, you contact a long-time supplier that sells the parts needed to fill the order, and you purchase the parts. But when the following week ends, you still haven't received the official order from TechInc. You phone Marlon, your contact from TechInc, to find out what's going on. "Oh," he says. "Well, we need to have more internal discussion about whether we can move forward with this project. We'll send you the order if we want to proceed." You're forced to cancel the order you placed with the parts supplier—setting the stage for mistrust in a previously positive relationship.

Misunderstandings are all too common when managers are communicating internationally. However, by employing strategies to avoid cross-cultural gaffes and by understanding the four areas where misunderstandings are most likely to occur (language, non-verbal communication, negotiation, and forms of agreement), you can improve the odds of success in your international business dealings.

Tips and Tools

Tools for
Managing Diversity

Understanding Interpersonal Bias

Use this tool to understand how being treated with prejudice feels and to appreciate the importance of discouraging prejudice and stereotyping in the workplace.

When you were shown prejudice:

Describe a situation in which someone showed prejudice toward you at work in the space below.

How did the incident make you feel?

How did you respond?

How might you have responded differently?

When you were prejudiced toward someone else:

Describe a situation where you think that you may have treated someone else in the workplace with prejudice.

How do you think the situation made the other person feel?

If the situation negatively affected your relationship with the other person, what steps might you take to repair the damage?

Creating an Inclusive Environment Self-Assessment

Use this tool to assess your ability to create a workplace environment in which all of your employees feel included and able to contribute their best on the job. For each statement below, indicate on a scale of 1 to 5 how strongly you agree or disagree with the statement. A "1" means "strongly disagree"; a "5" means "strongly agree."

| | Rating | | | | |
| | Low | | | High | |
Statement	1	2	3	4	5
1. I listen to all of my employees' concerns.					
2. I invite all of my employees to meetings during which decisions will be made that affect them or their work.					
3. I inform all of my employees about issues affecting them or their work.					
4. I make everyone in my department feel welcome.					
5. I treat all of my direct reports in ways that enable them to do their best work.					
6. My subordinates create value for our organization by engaging their knowledge and experience toward innovating, solving problems, and serving the organization's mission.					
7. I encourage my employees to contribute their skills, abilities, and unique knowledge and experience to contribute to the success of our department as well as the company.					
8. I trust my employees.					
9. My direct reports trust one another.					
10. My subordinates feel that they can "be themselves" at work.					
11. I demonstrate my appreciation for, and actively seek out, my employees' perspectives on the projects and efforts we're working on in our department.					

Statement	Rating				
	Low				High
	1	2	3	4	5
12. My employees feel a sense of "belonging" in the department and feel some ownership of and investment in our efforts.					
13. I speak up when one or more of my employees are being excluded during discussions.					
14. When I disagree with a direct report, I ask for their thoughts and experiences and accept their frame of reference as true for them.					
15. With employees whose primary language is different from my own, I learn how to say a few words in their language.					

Next Steps

For each statement where you rated your agreement as "1" or "2," list ideas for improving your ability in that area.

Statement number:	Ideas for improving:

Creating a Diversity Profile

Use this worksheet to create a staff diversity profile. Under each category, write the number of employees who fit each description. After developing this profile, identify ways to maximize the diversity of your team.

Part I: Developing Your Profile

Date of profile:

Department or team:

Age	Gender
Mature workers (age 56+) _____ Midage workers (age 37–55) _____ Young workers (age 20–36) _____	Male _____ Female _____ Transgendered _____

Race/Ethnicity	**Physical/Cognitive Ability**
African American/Black _____ Asian Indian _____ Asian _____ Polynesian _____ Latino/Hispanic _____ White _____ Two or more races _____ Native American _____ Other _____	Employees with a physical disability _____ Employees with a cognitive disability _____

Personal Status	**Sexual Identity** *(for employees who are open about their identities)*
Domestic partnered _____ Domestic partnered with dependent(s) _____ Married _____ Married with dependent(s) _____ Single _____ Single with dependent(s) _____	Gay _____ Lesbian _____ Bisexual _____ Transgendered _____

Education	Religious Affiliation *(for employees who are open about* *their religious affiliation)*
Did not complete high school _____ Completed high school _____ Completed 2-year college _____ Completed 4-year college _____ Completed graduate degree _____ Completed doctorate _____	Christian _____ Other _____ Jewish _____ Muslim _____ Hindu _____ Buddhist _____ Agnostic/Atheist _____

Part II: Maximizing Your Team's Diversity

Diversity challenges in my department:	Ideas for addressing those challenges:
Diversity strengths in my department:	Ideas for building on those strengths:

Recruitment Interview Checklist

Use this checklist to ensure that you're prepared to answer important questions from diverse job candidates during the interviewing process. For each question below, fill in the answer if you know it. For questions whose answers you don't know, indicate how you will gather the information.

Date of interview:

Name of interviewee:

Interviewee's defining diversity characteristic (e.g., race, ethnicity, gender, age, etc.):

Candidate's Questions	Your Responses
How many people like me do you have in this organization?	
How many of the people like me are in middle and senior management positions?	
How many of the people like me are in professional or technical positions?	
What are my chances for progressing/advancing my career in this organization?	

Candidate's Questions	Your Responses
Do you have a formal mentoring program and/or career development programs for people like me and other diverse groups?	
What does this organization do in terms of community outreach efforts to partner with diverse groups?	
Do you have employee affinity groups that focus on the needs of people like me and other groups?	
Are managers in this organization trained to communicate and manage diverse employees?	
What initiatives, events, and programs has your organization participated in regarding diversity?	
Does the organization have formal diversity initiatives and programs in place?	

Cultural Intelligence Self-Assessment

Use this tool to identify aspects of your cultural intelligence (CI) that would benefit from strengthening. For each statement below, check "Yes" if you agree; "No" if you disagree. Then read the ideas for strengthening any weak areas.

CI Gained Through Thought and Observation

Statement	Yes	No
Before I interact with people from a new culture, I ask myself what I hope to achieve.		
If I encounter something unexpected while working in a new culture, I use this experience to figure out new ways to approach other cultures in the future.		
I plan how I'm going to relate to people from a different culture before I meet them.		
When I come into a new cultural situation, I can immediately sense whether something is going well or something is wrong.		

Strengthening weak areas:

For any statements where you checked "No," list ideas for strengthening that ability. For example, suppose you tend not to plan how you're going to relate to people from a different culture before you meet them. In this case, you might consider working with a coach before your next cross-cultural meeting, to familiarize yourself ahead of time with the other culture's business practices.

CI Gained Through Behavioral Mirroring

Statement	Yes	No
It's easy for me to change my body language (for example, eye contact or posture) to suit people from a different culture.		
I can alter my facial expression when a cultural encounter requires it.		
I can modify my speech style (for example, accent or tone) to suit people from a different culture.		
I easily change the way I act when a cross-cultural encounter seems to require it.		

Strengthening weak areas:

For any statements where you checked "No," list ideas for strengthening that ability. For example, suppose you have difficulty modifying your speech style or facial expression when cultural encounters require it. In this case, you could consider taking an acting class to strengthen your ability in this area.

CI Gained Through Motivation and Belief in Possibility		
Statement	Yes	No
I have confidence that I can deal well with people from a different culture.		
I am certain that I can befriend people whose cultural backgrounds are different from mine.		
I can adapt to the lifestyle of a different culture with relative ease.		
I am confident that I can deal with a cultural situation that's unfamiliar.		

Strengthening weak areas:

For any statements where you checked "No," list ideas for strengthening that ability. For example, suppose you lack confidence in your ability to deal with an unfamiliar cultural situation. In this case, you may be able to boost your confidence by talking with colleagues who had felt equally nervous about being in new cultural situations but who learned how to manage their nervousness.

Preparing for a Cross-Cultural Business Trip

Use this worksheet to document your learning about another country you'll be visiting to conduct business. By documenting what you know about that country's culture, you can be better prepared to interact with your counterparts during the trip.

Part I: Trip Specifics

Date of trip:

Country to be visited:

Purpose of visit:

Individual(s) I will meet with:

Cultural information sources to consult:

Part II: Document Your Findings

In the sections below, document what you learn about how people in the country you'll be visiting handle the following activities:

Greeting new business associates	Making decisions
Negotiating	Handling conflicts
Establishing deadlines	Disclosing personal information
Conducting meetings	Carrying out specific work processes

Interacting with authority figures	Using nonverbal signals
Acquiring knowledge	Entertaining business associates
Displaying status	Delivering presentations
Setting business priorities and goals	Selling and marketing to customers
Defining agreement on a business deal	Giving gifts
Discussing workplace accomplishments	Other

Test Yourself

This section offers ten multiple-choice questions to help you identify your baseline knowledge of the essentials of managing diversity. Answers to the questions are given at the end of the test.

1. What is diversity in an organization?

   a. Differences among employees in a workplace.

   b. Unit-level initiatives intended to improve job opportunities for women and people of color.

   c. Company-level policies governing the number of minority members a firm must employ to meet legal requirements.

2. Which of the following best defines *stereotypes*?

   a. Behavior intended to denigrate another person, based on his or her race, gender, or other distinguishing characteristic.

   b. Conventional, formulaic, and oversimplified conceptions, opinions, or images of particular groups.

   c. An adverse judgment or opinion formed beforehand or without knowledge or examination of the facts.

3. Jack, a newly hired African American marketing vice president, meets his company's executive team for the first time, all of whom are white. Instead of expressing interest in Jack's marketing expertise, the executives ask whether he'd like to head up the firm's new diversity committee. What harmful message have the executives *most* likely conveyed to Jack?

    a. They're concerned that he can't succeed in the marketing job.

    b. They don't respect the skills he brings to his new role.

    c. They view him as a token.

4. Which of the following is the best way to manage a diverse workforce?

    a. Hire diverse employees, then ask them to adhere to uniform codes of conduct defining how to look, act, and get ahead—to send the message that "we're all the same."

    b. Identify employees' diverse experiences and perspectives, and incorporate them into the way the company does business—to change things for the better.

    c. Celebrate differences by assigning diverse employees to niche customer segments distinguished by gender, race, age, ethnicity, and other defining characteristics.

5. You work in a company located in a small city where the population is mostly white. Likewise, your firm's workforce predominantly comprises white males in their forties. You're considering assembling a new, diverse team to develop ideas for innovative products for your firm. Which of the following diversity strategies would you use?

a. Assemble a team representing ethnicities and age groups that differ from white men in their forties.

b. Assemble a team populated primarily by women in their forties.

c. Assemble a team containing members from a broad range of ethnicities, ages, genders, and national origin, including forty-five-year-old white males.

6. You want to hire more diverse employees from your company's area. Which of the following strategies would help you achieve this goal?

a. Ask employee affinity groups to "sell" potential new hires on the advantages of working for your organization.

b. Post job advertisements in the most widely read newspapers in the region to boost your chances of reaching diverse candidates.

c. Attend career-day activities sponsored by the nearest colleges and universities in your area.

d. All of the above.

7. Marta has recruited several highly qualified diverse candidates into her team and wants to ensure that they remain with her company. Which of the following strategies would *best* help her retain valued diverse employees?

    a. On a quarterly basis, reward excellent performance with a weekend getaway for two at a luxurious retreat.

    b. Apply equal criteria for high performance when conducting employees' regularly scheduled performance appraisals.

    c. Offer flextime and telecommuting for subordinates who have job responsibilities that can be carried out at any time and from any location.

8. Which of the following statements about culture is true?

    a. Culture determines a person's beliefs, behaviors, and values.

    b. Culture exists primarily at the national level.

    c. Culture primarily affects how people conduct themselves during business negotiations.

9. Henry is about to travel abroad for an important negotiation. He wants to strengthen his cultural intelligence to boost his chances of success during the negotiation. Which of the following would *best* help him increase his CI?

    a. Find out what people in the country he'll be visiting believe about life and work in general, then strive to adopt those beliefs himself.

    b. Research cultural rules of the other country ahead of time and prepare himself to follow those rules when he meets with his negotiation counterparts.

c. Develop a plan for how to observe his counterparts' behaviors during his first few encounters with them, and emulate those behaviors during later stages in the negotiation.

10. Alyssa is preparing to take a year-long overseas assignment for her company. She knows that cross-cultural miscommunication typically occurs in four areas. In addition to nonverbal communication, negotiation, and beliefs about what constitutes agreement on a business deal, what other key area should Alyssa watch for possible miscommunication once she begins her assignment?

a. Confusion about language.

b. Misunderstandings about gift-giving practices.

c. Mistakes over use of people's surnames.

Answers to test questions

1, a. Differences among employees can include race, gender, ethnic background, physical and cognitive abilities, sexual orientation, religious beliefs, learning and work styles, body type, and work/life commitments. Differences can also be cultural—such as ways of greeting new business associates, negotiating, and resolving conflicts that are unique to each country, region within a country, organization, or group within an organization.

2, b. Stereotypes can be positive or negative—for example, "Asians are smart and hardworking," "Californians are laid-back when it comes to business," "Women have trouble with math," "Irish people love their drink," and "Americans are pushy negotiators." Assumptions that all members of a particular group are the same can have damaging consequences in the workplace if these assumptions cause managers to deprive employees of equal opportunities.

3, c. By ignoring Jack's marketing expertise and inviting him to head up the diversity committee, the white executives most likely have made Jack feel that they can't see past his skin color. Jack may conclude that he's being exploited as a token or that he will be pigeonholed into roles that relate only to race. African Americans subjected to this behavior may wonder whether their white supervisors and peers value their business expertise. The resulting mistrust may cause them to leave the company in search of more welcoming environments.

4, b. By incorporating employees' diverse experiences and perspectives into the way the company does business, managers implement an "inclusion" approach to diversity. Inclusion transcends two flawed, extreme approaches to managing diversity: assimilation and differentiation. Assimilation encourages everyone to adhere to universal codes of conduct defining how to look, act, and get ahead. Employees downplay their differences, preventing the organization from benefiting from their unique perspectives. Differentiation assigns diverse employees to niche customer segments, which can make some people feel they're being pigeonholed or exploited as tokens.

5, c. The best diversity initiatives encompass *all* employees—not just members of minority groups. Before you implement any diversity initiative, it's important to ask yourself, "Will this initiative contribute to everyone's success on my team? Or will it produce an advantage for only one or certain groups?" The most valuable diversity initiatives benefit *everyone.*

6, d. Employee affinity groups can not only help you reach qualified diverse job candidates, but may also persuade them to accept an offer. For example, a "people of color" group could talk with candidates as well as community and educational organizations about your company, what it's like to work there, and how they've advanced in the firm. These groups help support the message to candidates "We value diversity here." Posting job advertisements in widely read newspapers in the region can help you reach additional promising candidates, as can attending career-day activities sponsored by local colleges and universities.

7, c. Tailoring work/life programs to employees' diverse needs and circumstances can help Marta retain talent. For example, for employees who are shouldering responsibility for their immediate *and* extended family, flextime and telecommuting can save them from burnout—and win their loyalty to Marta's company.

8, a. A person's culture strongly influences his or her beliefs about how the world works and how people should interact; behaviors including gestures, use of eye contact, facial expressions, and gift-giving rituals; and values—what the person considers most important—such as family or personal life, career, religious identity, and social responsibility.

9, b. By consulting books, articles, videos, DVDs, and other information sources before his trip, Henry could learn about the other country's cultural rules regarding greeting, entertaining, and negotiating. He could also get help from a coach specializing in cultural diversity, as well as foster relationships with people from the other country if possible. By learning about the other country's cultural rules, he can emulate them when meeting with his negotiation counterparts—thus demonstrating his esteem for them and for how they conduct business in their country. Such demonstrations encourage trust and openness—essential ingredients in any business interaction.

10, a. Often, people from different countries use English to discuss business together. But because comprehension of English can vary, misunderstandings of words and expressions may occur.

To Learn More

Articles

Earley, P. Christopher, and Elaine Mosakowski. "Cultural Intelligence." *Harvard Business Review*, October 2004.

This article examines the misunderstandings that can arise between people who are doing business together but who come from different cultures. The authors identify three sources of cultural intelligence: "head" (or rote learning about other cultures), "body" (mirroring the customs and gestures of people from other cultures), and "heart" (believing that one has the ability to understand people from unfamiliar cultures). They also offer a six-step process for cultivating cultural intelligence.

Ely, Robin J., Debra E. Meyerson, and Martin N. Davidson. "Rethinking Political Correctness." *Harvard Business Review* OnPoint Enhanced Edition, September 2006.

The authors' research shows that political correctness (PC) is a double-edged sword. Although it has helped many employees feel unlimited by their race, gender, or religion, the PC rule book can hinder people's ability to develop effective relationships across race, gender, and religious lines. Companies need to equip workers with skills—not rules—for building these relationships. When people treat their cultural differences—and related conflicts and tensions—as opportunities to gain a more accurate view of themselves, one another, and the situation, trust builds, and relationships become stronger. Leaders should put aside the PC rule book and instead model and encourage risk taking in the service of building the organization's relational capacity.

Harvard Business School Publishing. "Required Reading for White Executives, 2nd Edition." *Harvard Business Review* OnPoint Collection, 2005.

The four articles in this collection shed light on crucial aspects of diversity—including the mistrust and low expectations that many minority professionals sense coming from their white counterparts, the advantages that an integration approach to diversity holds over assimilation and differentiation, strategies for mentoring minorities, and ways to take minorities' unique experiences gained through community work. The articles are "Dear White Boss . . ." by Keith A. Caver and Ancella B. Livers; "Making Differences Matter: A New Paradigm for Managing Diversity" by David A. Thomas and Robin J. Ely; "The Truth About Mentoring Minorities: Race Matters" by David A. Thomas; and "Leadership in Your Midst: Tapping the Hidden Strengths of Minority Executives" by Sylvia Ann Hewlett, Carolyn Buck Luce, and Cornel West.

Rifkin, Glenn. "Building Better Global Managers." *Harvard Management Update*, March 2006.

Though strides have been made in developing successful global managers, it is a sad truth that too many companies assume that they can do things abroad in the same manner as they do them domestically. As a result, most managers still lack the necessary cultural awareness when dealing with overseas employees and partners, as well as the experience of managing increasingly complex processes long distance. Learn the steps leaders can take to develop in prospective global managers the "empathic qualities" necessary for working with individuals and systems that are unlike their own.

Rosenbaum, Andrew. "How to Steer Clear of Pitfalls in Cross-Cultural Negotiations." *Harvard Management Communication Letter*, March 2003.

Negotiation is always a delicate business. But it's doubly so when the person across the table comes from across the globe. Rosenbaum maintains that careful preparation can help managers anticipate danger zones and navigate around them. The author offers several suggestions: (1) *Understand expectations* about how decisions will be made (by individuals or through consensus) and how much leeway the negotiators will have to change a decision once it's made. (2) *Establish a problem-solving approach* by trying to get as much as you can without handing out a deal breaker and by finding common ground wherever possible. (3) *Manage the negotiation*, understanding and working with your counterpart's cultural style.

Thomas, David A. "Diversity as Strategy." *Harvard Business Review*, September 2004.

Thomas provides a wealth of examples of how diverse task forces have generated profitable ideas for IBM—presenting a compelling business case for diversity. He also traces IBM's diversity task force initiative, from its roots in 1995 (soon after Lou Gerstner became CEO) through the challenges and successes that have come since then. IBM created eight diversity task forces (Asians, blacks, people with disabilities, white men, women, gays/lesbians/bisexuals/transgender individuals, Hispanics, and Native Americans), each of which focused on distinct business priorities. For example, the women's task force concentrated on networking and work/life balance, among other issues. And the Native American task force focused on recruiting and community outreach.

Books

Fields, Martha R. A. *Indispensable Employees: How to Hire Them, How to Keep Them*. Franklin Lakes, NJ: Career Press, 2001.

Fields offers several chapters focused on the unique challenges of recruiting and retaining diverse workers. In one chapter, she lays out the business case for diversity and links it to global business trends and shifting workforce demographics. Tips follow for recruiting and retaining diverse employees, creating a staff diversity profile, and answering key questions from diverse job candidates. Case studies show how several companies have successfully strengthened and leveraged diversity in their workforces. Additional chapters offer advice for managing workers of different age groups, work styles, and work/life commitments.

Harvard Business School Press. *Harvard Business Review on Managing Diversity*. Boston: Harvard Business School Press, 2001.

This collection of classic and cutting-edge articles, case studies, and first-person perspectives provides a broad range of perspectives on affirmative action, career development for minorities and women, and other diversity-related topics. Contents include "From Affirmative Action to Affirming Diversity" by R. Roosevelt Thomas Jr.; "A Modest Manifesto for Shattering the Glass Ceiling" by Debra Meyerson and Joyce K. Fletcher; "Mommy-Track Backlash" by Alden M. Hayashi; "Two Women, Three Men on a Raft" by Robert Schrank; "Winning the Talent War for Women: Sometimes It Takes a Revolution" by Douglas M. McCracken; and "Is This the Right Time to Come Out?" by Alistair D. Williamson.

Rasmussen, Tina. *The ASTD Trainer's Sourcebook: Diversity*. New York: McGraw-Hill, 1996.

Rasmussen offers materials helpful for managers interested in delivering diversity workshops in their organizations. Materials include customizable training designs, fully reproducible workshop documents, games, questionnaires, group activities, overhead masters, and participant handouts. Prepared by experts at the top of their fields on behalf of the American Society for Training and Development, the resources in this volume should be helpful for managers in large and small organizations alike.

Rokes, Beverly. *Embracing Diversity*. Quick Skills Series. Cincinnati: South-Western Educational Publishing/Thomson Learning, 2001.

This concise, handy volume analyzes the benefits of diversity and provides a wealth of information and exercises for maximizing the value of a diverse workforce. Topics include learning about other cultures, showing respect, helping others fit into your organization, communicating across genders and cultures, handling diversity-related conflicts, and working abroad (including serving international customers).

eLearning Programs

Harvard Business School Publishing. *Managing Difficult Conversations*. Boston: Harvard Business School Publishing, 2001.

This program will help you understand why disagreements occur and help you build conclusions collaboratively. These productive dialogue skills will lead to a more accurate, shared understanding of the information exchanged in your daily interactions. *Managing Difficult Conversations* examines techniques for approaching and handling difficult business conversations. The program explores how mental models influence our private thinking and, thus, our behavior. It presents the Left-Hand Column exercise as a technique for unveiling and examining our internal thought process. The program also examines five unproductive thinking habits that many people fall into during difficult conversations and five productive alternative ways of thinking. By examining your own thinking habits and actively seeking more productive mind-sets, you can learn to approach difficult conversations with confidence, avoid blaming, overcome defensiveness, and make better business decisions.

Harvard Business School Publishing. *Productive Business Dialogue.* Boston: Harvard Business School Publishing, 2002.

This program shows managers how to craft conversations that are fact based, minimize defensiveness, and draw out the best thinking from everyone involved. *Productive Business Dialogue* introduces the Ladder of Inference, a tool that helps participants in a dialogue understand the distinctions among fact, interpretation, and conclusions and how making these distinctions clear can dramatically enhance the productivity of meetings and discussions. Through interactive, real-world scenarios, you will practice shaping interactions that maximize learning and lead to better-informed decisions.

Other Information Sources

www.diversitybestpractices.com

This member-based service enables corporations and public-sector organizations to exchange best practices related to diversity challenges and to share diversity management tips and resources.

www.multiculturaladvantage.com

On this site, visitors will find a wealth of information on workforce diversity and the opportunity to receive a free newsletter.

www.hirediversity.com

This online service provides information and strategies for recruiting diverse employees and supporting their career development.

www.tolerance.org

Visitors to this site will find information on how to dismantle bigotry and create communities that value diversity.

Sources for Managing Diversity

The following sources aided in development of this book:

Alon, Ilan, and James M. Higgins. "Global Leadership Success Through Emotional and Cultural Intelligences." *Business Horizons* 48 (2005).

Caver, Keith A., and Ancella B. Livers. "Dear White Boss . . ." *Harvard Business Review* OnPoint Enhanced Edition, November 2002.

Diversity Trends LLC. "Powerful Partnerships: Maximizing Return on Investment with Affinity Groups." 2001.

Earley, P. Christopher, and Elaine Mosakowski. "Cultural Intelligence." *Harvard Business Review*, October 2004.

Ely, Robin J., Debra E. Meyerson, and Martin N. Davidson. "Rethinking Political Correctness." *Harvard Business Review* OnPoint Enhanced Edition, September 2006.

Fields Associates, Inc. "Handling Differences Using the Fields Associates JOB-IT Model." 2006.

Fields Associates, Inc. "My Staff Diversity Demographic Profile Exercise." 2006.

Fields, Martha R. A. *Indispensable Employees: How to Hire Them, How to Keep Them*. Franklin Lakes, NJ: Career Press, 2001.

Fields, Richard, Dr. "How Managers Can Enhance Their Effectiveness by Creating and Sustaining an Inclusive Workplace Environment."

Fondon, Janine. "From Impression to Impact: Five Most Web-Inspiring Ways to Recruit and Retain Diverse Professionals and Wow Consumers and Communities of Color." *Business World Index*, December 6, 2006, UnityFirst.com.

Gardenswartz, Lee, and Anita Rowe. "Savvy Managers Tune in to Cultural Differences." *Managing Smart*, Summer 2001.

Gordon, Jack. "Diversity as a Business Driver." *Training*, May 2005.

Harvard Business School Publishing. *Managing Across Difference*. Boston: Harvard Business School Publishing, 2003.

———. "Required Reading for White Executives, 2nd edition." *Harvard Business Review* OnPoint Collection, 2005.

Hewlett, Sylvia Ann, Carolyn Buck Luce, and Cornel West. "Leadership in Your Midst: Tapping the Hidden Strengths of Minority Executives." *Harvard Business Review* OnPoint Enhanced Edition, November 2005.

Johansson, Frans. "Masters of the Multicultural." *Harvard Business Review*, October 2005.

Mor Barak, Michalle E. *Managing Diversity: Toward a Globally Inclusive Workplace*. Thousand Oaks, CA: Sage Publications, Inc., 2005.

Rifkin, Glenn. "Building Better Global Managers." *Harvard Management Update*, March 2006.

Rokes, Beverly. *Embracing Diversity*. Quick Skills Series. Cincinnati: South-Western Educational Publishing/ Thomson Learning, 2001.

Rosenbaum, Andrew. "How to Avoid Being the 'Ugly American' When Doing Business Abroad." *Harvard Management Communication Letter*, December 2002.

———. "How to Steer Clear of Pitfalls in Cross-Cultural Negotiation." *Harvard Management Communication Letter*, March 2003.

Thomas, David A. "Diversity as Strategy." *Harvard Business Review*, September 2004.

———. "The Truth About Mentoring Minorities: Race Matters." *Harvard Business Review* OnPoint Enhanced Edition, April 2001.

Thomas, David A., and Robin J. Ely. "Making Differences Matter: A New Paradigm for Managing Diversity." *Harvard Business Review* OnPoint Enhanced Edition, September–October 1996.

Thomas, R. Roosevelt. "From Affirmative Action to Affirming Diversity." *Harvard Business Review* OnPoint Enhanced Edition, March–April 1990.

Notes

Notes

Notes

Notes

Notes

Notes

Notes

Notes

How to Order

Harvard Business Press publications are available worldwide from your local bookseller or online retailer.

You can also call:
1-800-668-6780

Our product consultants are available to help you 8:00 a.m.–6:00 p.m., Monday–Friday, Eastern Time. Outside the U.S. and Canada, call: 617-783-7450.

Please call about special discounts for quantities greater than ten.

You can order online at:
www.HBSPress.org

Notes

Notes

Notes

Notes

Notes

Notes

How to Order

Harvard Business Press publications are available worldwide from your local bookseller or online retailer.

You can also call:
1-800-668-6780

Our product consultants are available to help you 8:00 a.m.–6:00 p.m., Monday–Friday, Eastern Time. Outside the U.S. and Canada, call: 617-783-7450.

Please call about special discounts for quantities greater than ten.

You can order online at:
www.HBSPress.org